This book is a presentation of Weekly Reader
Books. Weekly Reader Books offers book
clubs for children from preschool through high
school. For further information write to:
WEEKLY READER BOOKS, 4343 Equity Drive,
Columbus, Ohio 43228

This edition is published by arrangement
with Checkerboard Press.

Weekly Reader is a federally registered trademark
of Field Publications.

Why Is It Cold?

A **Just Ask**™ Book

Hi, my name is Christopher!

by Chris Arvetis
and Carole Palmer

illustrated by
Vernon McKissack

FIELD PUBLICATIONS
MIDDLETOWN, CT.

I can show you more about cold weather with my weather map.
We can find out where our cold weather begins.
Look at the X.

Cold air and strong winds make us feel cold.

This gadget tells us how hard the wind is blowing.

The harder the wind blows, the colder it feels.

Sometimes the cold air causes clouds to form in the sky.
Water in the clouds gets colder and colder.
It often turns to ice.
When the ice gets heavy, it falls to the earth as snow.

Many clouds in the sky keep the sun from shining on us. Without the sun, the temperature drops lower and lower.

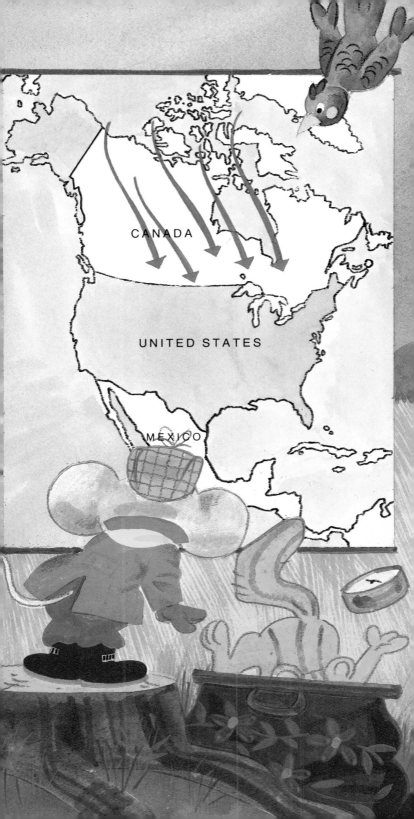

CANADA

UNITED STATES

MEXICO

The temperature drops lower and lower.